Sexting

Sexting
by Clementine Morrigan

Published by Clementine Morrigan
Montréal, Québec

clementinemorrigan.com

Copyright © Clementine Morrigan 2021

All rights reserved. No part of this book may be reproduced or transmitted in any form without permission from the author, with the exception of brief excerpts used for the purposes of promotion or review.

ISBN 978-1-988178-02-8

Layout and design by Elen Kolev
Cover illustration by Marta Gómez Hervás
Cover design by Jay Marquis-Manicom

Also by Clementine Morrigan

Rupture (2012)
The Size of a Bird (2017)
You Can't Own the Fucking Stars (2018)
Trauma Magic (2021)
Fucking Magic (2021)

Sexting

*For the sluts, the queers,
and the hopeless romantics.*

Pain

Danger

We are watching apocalypse unfold in real time
on our smartphones

We are caught in the freeze response of our
parasympathetic nervous systems

Cycling between grief and rage and panic
numbness and despair

I feel your body, it is warm like an animal
I tell you about the phragmites taking over the
　river

We fuck, we lie in each other's arms
We wonder what it would take to change things

We are safe together
We are in so much danger

Ghosted

I want a safe place for my desire
The accumulated trauma of hook up culture
Ghosted, haunted, hunted, he picks me up
puts me on his lap when I say
I have to leave

Stay awhile, we can just talk
I didn't mean it like that
Now you're making me feel
like I did something wrong
Can we start over?

He lives in his mother's basement
He rips my only pair of fishnets
I walk home sick smelling of his sweat

Courage

Before I know it
he is unbuttoning my jeans

his fingers searching for a wetness which
has not arrived

For a second I let him but my mind is a siren
You can't do this to yourself again

With all the courage I have
I remove his hand

Bisexual

I mean technically I'm still bisexual
but I am exhausted by the trauma of
trying to date heterosexual men

It is finally outweighing the trauma of
internalized homophobia

Textbook

Incest survivors exhibit
higher rates of self-injury
addiction promiscuity
suicide attempts autoimmune
disorders
repeated sexual assaults and
experiences of domestic
violence

Wet

I choose rejection in order to reject myself
I abandon my body in the woods and
chase down love in the city
I am famished

My hunger takes on new proportions
I look you in the eye like a dog begging
I am powerless over my need and

you are repelled by it

I am turned on by hard surfaces
I don't get hard, don't feel any hardness in myself
I don't know that I am hot until
I find that I am sweating
I don't feel any pleasure but I am soaking wet

He whispers in my ear
you are dripping

I chase down love, running through the city
I throw myself down at the threshold of your
 door
I make a wooden sign, a giant billboard

It reads *LOVE ME*

You are surprised by this, I am so easy

I press my body against your hardness
I drink cum and go numb

Ache

I find her instagram and stare at the pictures
I scroll through expensive lingerie
fingering my credit card

I go outside, the sidewalk is wet
the trees are bright with rain

I take a selfie in the mirror, send it to a couple
  people
I try to let the emojis I receive in response
  reassure me

I am hungry I am famished I am seeking myself

I find her instagram and I stare at the pictures
I don't want to be her but I want to be free of this
  ache

Anxious

Anxious preoccupied attachment
in the age of social media

I refresh the feed, memorize numbers
Safety is a feeling that slips away so easily

There is so much data but I discount
what doesn't fit my narrative

I am selective and I am focused on danger

Security isn't a place that I arrive
Love isn't something I can earn or bargain for

When I am anxious I am not available
When I am preoccupied I am not present

I am not here

Need

A poem cannot contain the desire
I felt for you, hot sharp unspoken
forbidden, not by anyone in particular
but we knew

We were playing with fire
We moved in the dark
Your hand on my neck

This is more than fucking could ever be
This is more than being under water
More than needing to breathe

Lovers

You break up with me casually
over crackers and hummus

I was talking to him today and he said
he might not be into this polyamory thing
and I asked myself Would I go monogamous
for the guy? I think I would

You say it like I am your bestie
like we are friends and not lovers
like we haven't been dating for more
than a year

Agential

I am both hunter and prey
both famished and feeding

Falling down at the altar
collapsed on the floor
I don't cry anymore

I don't drink, I don't cut myself
or take too many pills

I spend seven hours staring
at a small screen in my hand

I go into the moving water
of the river and I feel nothing

I don't make myself cum
I don't touch my own pussy

I am afraid of the end of the world
There isn't enough time

I am both anxious and agential
I disavow my power in elaborate
acts of ritual

I am afraid of who I am in love
who I am in need

Presence

Unavailable

I know I love her but I don't tell her
I let her kiss me outside the metro
I let her tell me goodbye

I know I love her but I don't tell her
She is *unavailable* and *avoidant*
and so am I

Dilate

My desire is to pay attention
The one thing I don't have is a body
Sink into the bed, my fingers trace
an outline, a memory of a fantasy
a conjuring

I want to show you my skeleton, my ghost
I want to show you an apparition
Evidence of something that is not here

Here, your fingers in my mouth
My fingers tracing the edge of your lips
You suck me in, your pupils dilate

Here you crack me open and my spirit
comes flying out of my skin
It goes drifting out through the window
I want to jam it back inside of me
I want to make it stay

Summer

I lie in the tall grass by the train tracks
The sky summerblue bright
The sun on my psoriasis legs sprawled
my dress hiked up

I want to write a whole book about pleasure
without mentioning rape
I want to lie in the sun in the grass
shading my eyes and reading my favourite
poetry book

I want to be like a plant, no one asks what a
plant is doing by the train tracks
but everyone stops to stare at a rabbit

The rabbit freezes and runs

Anchor

I press my pussy into the river bank
My toes find the shock of cold water
My skin hot in the summer sun

The bone of my pussy presses into the earth
which both pushes back and yields to me

I am kissing you, I am watching myself
embodied, disembodied

I anchor myself to the water, the river
the wet earth holding me here
with you

Dialectic

Compulsive sexuality
cock sucking, remember when I
would guzzle cum and get off on it or

Numbness, disinterest
My body nonresponsive

I feel nothing

Cum

I can't feel anything when anyone
touches my clit *Do you think that means you're
dissociating?* I hadn't thought about it

A pervasive numbess, a fast car no brakes
A touch like a ghost, it isn't *right*, it isn't
there

Here, I open into the green, your mouth
warm with breath that moves inside you
You are an animal, I am an animal
This is wet like tongue and spit

I cum like a shudder, like a prayer of surrender
I cum like a thundercloud finally releasing
rain

Now

White walls, the tangle
of your bedsheets, the light
clear and undiluted

The ease of your smile
This moment will pass

I will remember it
but it won't be the same
as living it now

Desire

Gay

Do you want me to fuck you
with my hand or strap it on?

Do you want to go
to this poetry reading?
We could or we could just
cuddle up in bed

you could read me your smutty stories

(It doesn't turn me on
when he says *you look so innocent*

It doesn't turn me on
when he asks me if I'll suck his cock

and then informs he won't

eat my pussy because we just met

He says: You say you're gay
so why do you want to fuck me?
I mean, you said you're gay
so I assumed you don't get fucked

You said you're gay
so assumed you don't suck cock)

Is there anything I should know?
Is there any way you don't
like to be touched?

How will you let me know
if you want to stop?

(All I can do is laugh,
walk home in a slutty dress
feeling like a fag)

Scissoring

The next day my pussy is bruised
where yours smashed into mine

The desperate clawing closeness
All angle and pressure

We are driving into each other
with the force
of desire

You are fucked up beautiful lying
beneath me

You laugh it off

You say there is shame that comes up
when you call yourself
a pillow princess

But I could fuck you all day like this

Nudes

I send you nudes like they are poems
The warmth of my flesh made digital

The touch of your fingers against me
as my fingers move across my phone

Swipe

374 matches on tinder
swipe left, swipe right, congratulations
I have a new match, you
are the last person I fucked in my bed
you are the last person I fucked
in this city, in that city
your hip bones where you told me to lick
your hands on the back of my head
mine folded in my lap
where you told me to put them

Drool

I am not worried, my mouth is a chalice
Neither blood nor wine but spit
Clear wet and abundant, I pour forth
Drooling all over your chair, creating
an opening, a container, a passageway
I have no fear, no hope, only presence
I have no time, no sequence, only now
The snow is wet becoming rain like
my body the world is made new again

Compelled

Both the page and my body do not respond
to just anything

It's not the fingers making shapes but
the depth of feeling beneath them

Breath held I await an entrance

It's not enough to want, I must be
compelled

Down, to the place where my forehead
touches the bathroom floor

When I am ordered to stand
and face the wall

I can't see you but I know you are here

Refusal

She takes my hand
She kisses me in public

Men scream at us from passing cars
Make it sexy girls

We work so hard
to find a space for us

A space where our bodies
find each other, from the inside

where desire roots
and grows, without imposition

where pleasure spreads like refusal

wild and unafraid

Happiness

The horses run toward the water
their muscled bodies liquid with movement
their round eyes full of light and pleasure

My body on the tiled bathroom floor
has lost its spirit

I lie here and remember the horses
their unencumbered freedom
their unbridled joy

He calls me pretty from the passenger side
    window
trying to get my number while driving and
    smoking
multitasking awkwardly and impressively

Just in case this is my chance at happiness
I tell him my phone number twice

Desire

It is unbelievably brave to want
I turn toward and not away from desire

which has no shape

It is shapeless like the water spilling always
   outside
of any boundary erected to contain it

When I discovered desire I was repelled by it
sickened by my capacity to want
humiliated

You sit between my legs, my lover, my friend
I show you through fits of shame
which I crush with all my strength

how to touch me with my vibrator
how to make me cum

Love

Precious

You're a slut and all you ever wanted
was to be respected, all you ever wanted
was for someone to love you
as you are, covered in cum and desperate
for dick, you are loved, you are precious

Balaclava

You can't be my mother or my father
Your love sweet and undeniable
Absent, I trace my fingers along an
outline, I am finding a way in

I break into my body, break and enter
fast in the middle of the night
before I have time to wake up and sound
an alarm, call for help, I climb in
through the window all balaclava and
stealth, all crowbar and intent

You are the unspoken words, the
waiting, the way my body leans in
when I like it, more of that please
Pulls away when it's too much
Not there, not so direct, you
are the silences, the things I can't say
like yes please, like I want this
like please don't fucking stop
like please don't go away

Stranglehold

Flesh soft, spread
like a bruise, my bones bend
Marrow all space, holding
breath, expanding and
contracting to the sound
of your name on my tongue

It is a stranglehold, sharp edge
Dangerous the way I lean into desire
Body vulnerable, like a little lock
for a little key, the shape of an
open palm, a throat exposed

Belly up I am a whale
I am the weakness of want
Your picture makes me
gasp for air like a fish but I can't
admit it, flesh stretched like
a balloon about to burst, my body
tense but softening, the shiver of
adrenaline gives way to the pleasure
of surrender, I have already lost

Longer

My hand against your hair
shaved close to your skull

In sleep, your hand reaches
for mine, holds it

The bruises you press
into my skin, sweet

I push my fingers into them
to keep them longer

Purple

Discerning yet reckless
Splayed, torn open, my
bruise purple the colour
made from your mouth
Bone against bone, blood
blooming like roses
Eyes rolled back, relentless
You come for me

Sacred

If it wasn't illegal I'd fuck you right here
you tell me on the metro platform
I am looking at you wide eyed as
electric currents move between us

In your bed sweat and hunger
Longing unfurls into touching
Your hands are a prayer and I am praying
Here where being a slut is a sacred act

Tendrils

I feel my body relax
I'm all tendrils and limbs

Spit and warmth and contorted shapes
softness

I am open, like a shell but I am
squishy like the creature that left it

Blood pumps, quarts of it
hot in my veins, I'm melting

You open your hand and I drink from it
like a little cat

Sexting

Cold coffee and condom wrappers
Bed head for days and sex for hours

Remember when we fell in love over
facebook messenger, remember when you
were a seven hour bus ride away

Remember when the CN Tower was my
compass, the centre, the heart
I would walk through the market
the pigeons would fly into the sky
I texted to say it's laundry day
I texted to say here's a selfie

You texted to say get out of my head
You texted to say you miss me

Your presence here in my arms
Your presence in your absence
in a little text bubble on my phone

Right

My therapist accused me
of falling in love with you
after the first time
we hooked up

I laughed it off
I'm not in love, I said
I barely knew you but

my therapist was right

Familiarity

Love takes the shape of spacetime
bending, I fall like a planet toward the sun
caught in orbit but not like a planet

I am an electron, I am everywhere and
nowhere at once

I love you and I am aging, I am growing
to love you more in our familiarity

I am safer and more afraid
I have everything to lose and I am fearless

Naked in your bed our bodies find each other
We touch each other expertly and there is
so much we don't know

Revelation

I wanted to write a love poem
but instead I travelled back in time
to rescue the twelve year old girl I was

I wanted to surrender myself
to the practice of devotion
but instead I found myself
alive and waiting for my own return

I wanted to love you so that
I could forget about the love
I wasn't given when I needed it the most

So that I could abandon the work
of meeting myself

Instead I found that love is reckoning

In order to meet you I had to meet myself
In order to know you I had to know myself

I wanted the reward of love
the final arrival, the exhale

but the breath is always moving

and love is more revelation
than reward

Clementine Morrigan is a writer. She wrote the books *Rupture*, *The Size of a Bird*, *You Can't Own the Fucking Stars*, *Trauma Magic*, and *Fucking Magic*. You can find more of her work at clementinemorrigan.com.

www.ingramcontent.com/pod-product-compliance
Lightning Source LLC
Chambersburg PA
CBRC091201070526
44579CB00008B/69